The Ant and the Carrot

Written by Narinder Dhami

Illustrated by Tomislav Zlatic

OXFORD
UNIVERSITY PRESS

OXFORD
UNIVERSITY PRESS

Great Clarendon Street, Oxford, OX2 6DP, United Kingdom

Oxford University Press is a department of the University
of Oxford. It furthers the University's objective of excellence
in research, scholarship, and education by publishing
worldwide. Oxford is a registered trade mark of Oxford
University Press in the UK and in certain other countries

British Library Cataloguing in Publication Data
Data available

ISBN: 978-0-19-841491-9

10 9 8 7 6 5 4

Paper used in the production of this book is a natural, recyclable product
made from wood grown in sustainable forests. The manufacturing process
conforms to the environmental regulations of the country of origin.

Printed in China

Acknowledgements

Series Editor: Nikki Gamble

The ant had a carrot.

But the carrot was big and long.

Then a rabbit got the carrot.

He bit off the top.

Then the rabbit met a fox.

The rabbit ran into the forest.

Then the fox had the carrot.

She bit off the end.

The farmer was in the shed.

She saw the fox.

The fox ran into her den.

All the ants had the carrot!